HOT OFF THE PRESS INC.

HOTP 2225

Making HERITAGE SCRAPBOOK PAGES

It's Easier Than You Think

Off to College 1946

Includes:
- 75 sam...
- guidel...
- 48 Pa...

(an $18.75 value)

Page Designers

We are grateful to the following people for creating the album pages which appear in this book. We're proud to feature their creative heritage album pages. In alphabetical order, they are:

- **LeNae Gerig** for Hot Off The Press, Inc.
- **Katie Hacker** for Hot Off The Press, Inc.
- **Linda Ipple**, Grand Rapids, Michigan

Production Credits

Project Manager: Teresa Nelson
Project Editors: Kris Andrews, Paulette Jarvey
Editors: Lynda Hill, Mary Margaret Hite
Photographer: John McNally
Graphic Designers: Carlee Justis, Jacie Pete
Digital Imagers: Victoria Gleason, Larry Seith

Manufacturers & Suppliers

The publisher would like to thank the following companies for providing tools and supplies used in this publication:

3L® for Memorabilia Pockets
Accu/Cut® Systems for die cuts
American Traditional Stencils for brass stencils
Artifacts, Inc. for doilies
Canson® for black, copper, silver and gold photo corners
ClearSnap for Top Boss embossing ink, Goldrush pigment ink and ColorBox® pigment ink
C.M. Offray & Son, Inc. for ribbon
Delta Technical Coatings, Inc. for alphabet stencil
DMD Industries for cardstock
EK Success Ltd. for colored pencils and pens, stickers and embossing powder
Family Treasures, Inc. for punches and pattern-edged scissors
Fiskars®, Inc. for pattern-edged scissors and black photo corners
Great Impressions® for rubber stamps
Hot Off The Press, Inc. for Paper Pizazz™ patterned papers, plain papers, and Paper Pizazz™ Punch-Outs™
Keeping Memories Alive™ for embossed photo mat
Lion Office for circle cutter
Marvy® Uchida for punches and pens
McGill, Inc. for punches, pens and pattern-edged scissors
Mrs. Grossman's Paper Company® for stickers
Rubber Stampede for rubber stamps
Stampendous!® for rubber stamps and embossing powder
Therm O Web for adhesive sticky dots
True Expressions™ for Magic Memories™ rub-ons
Zebra for metallic pens

published by:

HOT OFF THE PRESS INC.

©1999 by **HOT OFF THE PRESS** INC. All rights reserved. No part of this publication may be reproduced in any form or by any means, including photocopying, without permission in writing from the publisher. Printed in the United States of America.

While Hot Off The Press, Inc. guarantees Paper Pizazz™ papers and Punch-Outs™ to be acid-free (pH-correct), lignin-free and photo-safe, we cannot guarantee individual creative results. Therefore, Hot Off The Press, Inc. disclaims any liability for untoward results.

Hot Off The Press wants to be kind to the environment. Whenever possible we follow the 3 R's—reduce, reuse and recycle. We use soy and UV inks that greatly reduce the release of volatile organic solvents.

For a color catalog of nearly 750 products, send $2.00 to:

HOT OFF THE PRESS INC.

1250 N.W. Third, Dept. B
Canby, Oregon 97013
phone (503) 266-9102
fax (503) 266-8749
http://www.paperpizazz.com

Table of Contents

Researching Your Family History 5

This chapter brings insight and hints for making the research phase of creating your family's heritage album easier for you. With ideas on where to start presented in a frank, understandable manner, you'll be discovering your roots in no time.

Collecting Family Photos. 9

Collecting your family's photos is a very rewarding part of tracing your family's background. In this chapter you'll learn how to recognize and remove photos which were saved in unhealthy environments. You'll also find helpful ideas for organizing and storing all your photos.

Gathering Tools & Supplies 15

Preserving the integrity of your ancestors' photos is important—this chapter will explain how to do this while still using your favorite pattern-edged scissors, Punch-Outs™, punches, stickers and die cuts. You'll discover how colors and patterns in the papers you choose can highlight and enhance the tones and shading in all your photos.

The Basics of Scrapbooking 23

Review is good—even for the seasoned scrapper—but this chapter just may show you a new idea, too! This chapter includes the basic techniques of scrapbooking, layout principles and tips for creatively using heritage photos without cropping them, as well as cropping heritage photos with confidence. Also included are examples of journaling which will make writing your family's history a manageable task.

Bringing It All Together. 29

This chapter provides many ideas of how to bring all the photos, stories, | memorabilia and a ton of memories together into an impressive family heirloom— your heritage album. Using the papers found in this book and some of our other Paper Pizazz™ books, pages have been designed especially for heritage albums, with clever techniques for making the photos the most important elements.

Questionnaire 46

Glossary 48

Researching Your Family History

Many times, the thought of "building" or creating a heritage photo album can be very intimidating. Different types of heritage albums can be made, from documenting your own memories of one special person, to tracing your roots back as far as possible, then building the album around the results using photos, stories and documents or memorabilia.

This book addresses those albums in which photos, old and new, are stored creatively within photo-safe binders. We've included instructions on how to take care of photos, how to sort, store, organize and mount them onto acid-free, lignin-free papers and have given suggestions and options for creating the album pages themselves.

This book also includes techniques to create unique album pages, eliminating the possibility of all the pages looking the same, yet maintaining the integrity of your heritage photographs. While we haven't gone into great detail on exploring your roots or developing your family tree, we have provided solutions and options to situations unique to creating a heritage album. If you're interested in exploring and documenting your own genealogy there are sources to help you research your family tree on page 6.

Creating your own heritage album can be fun and exciting, involving exploring the stories surrounding your ancestors and distant relations. Our goal is to provide information that makes the task easy and enjoyable.

Addresses you can use to help
you in researching your family:

Internet Aids–
·www.ancestry.com
·www.worldroots.com
·www.lds.net

Federal Records–
Us Department of Commerce
Bureau of the Census
Pittsburgh, Kansas 66762

State Records–
Obtain a copy of "Where to Write
for Vital Records" by sending an
S.A.S.E. and $2.25 to:
Superintendent of Documents
Government Printing Office
Washington, D.D. 20402-9325
or visit them at–
www.cdc.gov/nchswww

Defining the Scope

As you gather your photos and memorabilia, decide how extensive you want the album to be. Are you interested in highlighting one person's life or do you want to document your family as far back in time as possible? Maybe you simply want to collect and organize the photos you have into albums for safe storage.

Establishing the parameters of the project will help determine how lengthy the process of creating the album will be. It will also give you a better idea of how many photos you actually will need. Without defining the scope of the project, it could take much more time than you've alloted.

Finding Photo's and Stories

Finding photos of your family members can be very exciting. You'll scour attics, sift through basements, search among boxes, talk to relatives and ask family friends about contributing whatever they may have.

Telephoning family or friends provides an opportunity to get immediate response about what they have, and what you'll still need to find. You can also use e-mail, the internet or send letters. Once you tell others what you're doing and looking for, you may be surprised at how much information and how many photos a relative actually has.

Sometimes family members won't part with their originals. However, usually they're happy to offer copies of their collection of ancestral items. Use a color-photocopier to capture all the shading found in black and white or sepia-toned photos; remember to use acid-free, lignin-free paper.

On rare occasions, a family member may not want to share treasured photos or stories. While it is frustrating, there are tips in this book to help create album pages with a minimum of photos.

Interviews

Getting the facts about your family is the first place to begin when tracing your heritage. Photos have little impact without names and traceable relations to connect them to you. When interviewing family members, ask for as many specific names, dates and places as they can remember. Ask your grandparents and older relatives to tell you any stories they were told as children. Their stories may provide a hint or a name they may not have otherwise remembered. Also, ask different relatives about the same family event. You'll get different perspectives and a combined version that may be closer to the truth.

Ask neighbors of your grandparents if they know any names of your relatives or if they have photos. Seek out cousins or step-relatives that were removed by divorce or immigration to find what information they may have.

Record any information you find immediately; write down their responses or take a tape recorder or video camera to record the interview. You could also send a cassette tape to a relative and ask them to record their answers to a questionnaire you provide.

If you use a tape recorder or video camera, make a copy of the tape as soon as possible. Use one to play and review; store the other in a sealed PVC-free plastic container, keeping it in the same environment as your photos.

Send questionnaires to relatives who live too far away to visit (we've provided suggestions for questions on page 46). Don't forget to send them an acid-free pen to use when filling it out so their written answers can be included in your heritage album.

Collecting Family Photos

Gathering the photos to be added to a heritage album can be very exciting—and part detective work. Interviews of family members, while presenting some of the lesser known ancestors' photos, can result in the discovery of unknown relatives. This may lead to even more photos from those previously unknown family members or friends.

When collecting photos to be used in a heritage album, you may find many photos already mounted in an album. Generally, if the photos aren't damaged, there's no reason to remove them. This album was created, and possibly journaled in, by one of your ancestors and is a family heirloom which may be better left alone. If you need a photo or a journaled piece from the album, make a color copy.

Along the way, you're sure to learn of many keepsakes too big to be included in your album. To enjoy those beautiful items, photograph them! Maybe it's a china cabinet that's been in the family for 150 years, or Grandpa's first car that's currently rusting away in Uncle Chuck's garage; all can be photographed, then those photos can be added to your album page designs.

A clever way to include small, dimensional keepsakes is to color photocopy them. Pieces of jewelry, such as pearls, brooches and watches, as well as fabric swatches, copy very well. Then store those items in archival boxes and use the copies for your pages. Store memorabilia separate from photos and negatives; any acidic content in the items could contaminate the photos and negatives.

Because of contaminants that may be on them, don't store antique specialty photos such as tintypes or daguerreotypes with your photos. They're very fragile and scratch easily; wrap them in a soft cotton cloth to protect them, then contact a genealogist to determine the best method for archiving them.

As you collect photos and memorabilia from your family's beginnings, you will soon discover that your history is more than just your past; it's your heritage.

Rescue & Removal of Photos

A photo that has yellowed, become brittle, been torn, worn very thin, has drastically faded or was affixed with tape should be moved to a safer environment. Before doing anything, consider the possibility that removing it from its current environment may cause more damage. First copy the photo, then carefully remove the photograph. Or, choose another way of preserving it, such as having it professionally copied or photographed while still in the book.

If any ancestral photos have been placed in magnetic albums (the kind with adhesive on the page and cellophane film over the top), remove them immediately. The glue and the plastic film can turn the photos brittle and discolor them. The best recommendation for removal is using the product Un-Do by Doumar Products. Remarkably, it can be used directly on photos without any damage; it temporarily neutralizes the adhesive long enough to remove the photo from the album. It works on other self-adhesive products such as stickers and tapes, but it does not affect glues.

Other solutions include using a thin spatula and carefully working it between the photo and the page to lift the photo. Or, try using waxed dental floss in a sawing motion to work it behind the photo. If these options don't work, cut through the backing around the photo edge and use the photo as it is. Even though the backing may be acidic, the photo has survived this long and trying to pull the backing off may destroy the photo.

Care of Photos & Negatives

There are many variables that will shorten the life of your photos and negatives; correct handling and storage are the keys to eliminating most of them. The first rule is to wash your hands before handling any photos or negatives as the oils from your skin will damage them. Store your photos in archival quality storage boxes or envelopes which are available at scrapbook supply, photography or stationery stores. Often shoe boxes or non-archival boxes contain lignin, a natural wood substance that causes paper and photos to turn yellow and brittle over time.

Photos and negatives are subject to damage by the residue left from processing, as well as heat, light, fingerprints, bug infestations, mold, mildew, humidity and water. They must be stored in a photo-friendly environment: dry, cool, climate-controlled air with little dust and few bugs. Sound a bit like your living room? It is! The environment you enjoy most is also best for your photos.

The negative of a print is more valuable than the actual print because it is affected by fewer damaging agents and reproduces and stores much better. A negative can provide countless prints all just as perfect as the first one. They should not be stored with photos, as any small amounts of chemical residue on the photos will contaminate and work to deteriorate negatives.

Digital cameras and electronic photos are popular and now affordable. While we can't predict the future, it's a safe bet to assume that we'll be able to convert our pictorial files to the new and improved technology as it is developed.

Protect your negatives in PVC-free plastic negative sleeves; they allow you easy visual access without having to touch each negative. Most sleeves have areas where you can record the basic "who" and "when" of the negatives. Store them in a 3-ring binder in an acid-free and lignin-free box that's kept separate from your photos.

Old, unprotected and dirty negatives of photos can be cleaned with special negative cleaning products available in most photography supply stores. Then slip them into archival sleeves. If you have irreplaceable ancestral photos, have negatives made so they may be archived as well.

Reproducing Photos

As you create your heritage album, you may come across a photo that you wish you had duplicated. Perhaps you'd like to provide other family members with photos of a shared ancestor, or make a second, smaller heritage album as a gift, or just can't bring yourself to crop or cut the photos. For instance, the frame on the photo, left, was too pretty to omit, so it was duplicated along with the photo to be included in the album. In addition, there are other photo media that you simply can't put in a scrapbook page design, such as a slide or 8mm film, but may be the only forms on which an ancestral image is found. Duplicating them is the perfect answer, and relatively easy for professionals. Whatever the cost may be, if the photo is important to you, it's worth it!

Slides or reel-to-reel 8mm films can be converted to photographs (or upgraded to VHS home videos) at a relatively low cost. Consult with local camera shops or photography studios to have this done. If preserving the film in its original form is important, make sure no permanent alterations will be done in the duplication process. Store them in PVC-free plastic movie or slide cases and keep them in a cool, dry environment.

If you already own the technology—a computer, scanner and a basic photo-enhancement program—it's very economical, and quite simple, too, to restore or duplicate photos yourself digitally.

If you have a photo you can't remove from an old album and want a copy of it, you can take the page or the entire album to a reputable photo shop to have them duplicate or remove it for you. Photographing old photos yourself is another option, but if your camera doesn't provide the best quality, check with a camera shop to rent equipment. It will also give you a valuable negative for future prints. The page above right features a technique where one person (or area) in the group photo is reproduced and enlarged. This better ilustrates the journaling and puts the focus on the "star" of the page.

Sorting & Storing Photos

As you organize your photos, you'll see a direction and focus for your album. Keeping a journal or list of what photos you have and where they will fit into your album may become invaluable as you begin creating the pages. Not only will it provide you with cohesive organization, you'll know the holes in time that need to be filled, photos to search for and branches of the family to contact.

The methods of organizing your photos depend on how you plan to arrange your album. Most people like to work chronologically, either from the present to the past or from past to present. Group your photos by family member; use a soft #2 pencil or photo pencil to write the names and dates on the back edges of the photos. Then put them in labeled acid-free, lignin-free envelopes. You can further organize each person by arranging their photos in the order of their lives—childhood, school years, marriage, parenthood, career and retirement.

Other organizational methods include by memorable events, such as fifty years of family Christmases or wedding photos from all the family members' marriages. Organizing by time line may group all the family photos from 1850 and before in one box, from 1850 to 1900 in another, then separate each decade as needed, depending on the number of photos. Regardless of your method, store your grouped photos in archival boxes or acid-free, lignin-free envelopes.

Find a place in your home where photos and keepsakes can be kept without being disturbed or moved. If you don't have a free tabletop to use, consider using a large, flat piece of cardboard to spread your photos on, then slide it under a bed when you're not working on them.

Memorabilia

Maybe you have a bit of lace from an ancestor's wedding dress or a report card from your grandfather's school. Other items might be draft papers, commissions and discharge papers from the Civil War. While you'll want to include these keepsakes in your albums, it may not be appropriate to glue them to pages. These items, as well as small fabric pieces such as an old handkerchief or a christening bonnet, can be included in the album by inserting them into PVC-free plastic pockets especially designed for this— like the piece of wrapping paper stored in a plastic pocket on this album page.

Letters, handwritten recipes, diplomas and birth and marriage certificates are just a few keepsakes you may want to include in an album. If they are large, slip each into its own page protector, then design a coordinating page with photos to be placed opposite it. If the originals can't be included, color copy them, reducing each as needed to fit the pages.

You can construct your own pocket on the page using coordinating paper, then slip the memento into the pocket such as was done on the album page at the left. Be sure the keepsake is acid-free. If not, color-photocopy it and include the copy in the album. Store the original in a safe environment with other memorabilia.

Gathering Tools & Supplies

Collecting the photos and stories of ancestors and relatives for your heritage album may have provided you with hours of fascinating discovery into your family. Before putting all that together in the album, supplies must be gathered. All materials which will be included in the album must be neutral in acidic properties. Although some memorabilia will contain acid, there are methods of including them without allowing any damage to surrounding photos.

The term "acid-free" actually refers to the pH-balanced condition of the products. Papers for scrapbooking should have a pH level of 7.5. In addition, they should contain an alkaline to neutralize or stop the transference of acids from photos and other materials within the album. Most safe supplies will be labeled "archival," "photo-safe" or "acid-free." Avoid using papers, pens, mounting and storage supplies which lack one of these labels.

Lignin, a natural substance found in plants, must be removed during the paper-making process to ensure a photo-safe paper product. As with the storage containers, all papers touching photos should be lignin-free.

Album Types & Styles

When determining what type album to use for your heritage album, also consider the size. Although photo-safe scrapbooks can be found in all shapes and sizes, the supplies to fill them cannot. The most readily available sizes are 8½"x11" and 12"x12".

One method of determining what size an album to use is to consider whether you'll be sharing copies of the album with other family members. If so, 8½"x11" pages are much easier and more economical to duplicate than the larger 12"x12" pages. Although the 12"x12" albums provide plenty of space for photos, many times the number of heritage photos is very limited, making the smaller size easier to work with. The papers we've included in this book are 8½"x11" and, to compensate for those who wish to make the larger albums, we've also provided ideas and layouts for using them in the larger format.

Next, consider the style of album you wish to use. We prefer the 3-ring binder type because of its versatility and the ease of organization within it. The pages can be created on background papers, then slipped into PVC-free page protectors. At that point, the pages can be moved and rearranged as needed during the construction of the album. When some long-lost photos of a relative turn up well after you've finished that section of the album, pages of those photos can be added with very little effort. Both 8½"x11" and 12"x12" sizes are available in the 3-ring binder format, as are the papers and page protectors.

Solid & Patterned Papers

The album size and style determines the papers which will be used. If a 3-ring binder style is chosen, the album pages can be built directly onto background papers, then slipped into page protectors. If a strap or post binder is used, the pages are designed onto the pages which have been included in the binder, using patterned and solid papers as accents, or are designed then attached to white sheets.

Using Color

Some people use color as a way to follow the family line. One color for backgrounds and accents will index the father's side, while another will index the mother's side of the family. This may work in some cases, but can be limiting. We prefer to use journaling to indicate the relationship within the family structure; it allows any color to be used with each photo.

When choosing colors for the background of each scrapbook page, first take into account the mood of the photo—formal, informal, playful, masculine, feminine,

PRIVATE
CHRISTIANSEN
Company K
97th Division
Infantry
1944

etcetera. Generally, the formal, somber and masculine photos will lead you toward dark colors. Informal, feminine or baby photos look good when mounted on lighter colors.

Once the mood is established, look at the tones within the photos to determine which colors to use. Because heritage photos are black and white or sepia tones, most often they are enhanced when contrasting colors are used.Burgundy and dark blue can add elegance to a formal black and white family portrait; pink, peach and light blue bring a cheerful look to informal black and white photos, especially the children's or baby photos.

Be sure papers are acid-free and lignin-free. If the papers aren't labeled as such, an acid-testing pen is available where scrapbook supplies are sold. Use it to determine the safety of unlabeled papers. Avoid using newsprint and construction paper. Many contain lignin, which can hasten photos to yellow and become brittle.

Of course, brown is a natural for the sepia tone photos, but adding cream, metallic gold, shades of peach, coral, tan and rust behind the photos brings a richness to the album page. The formal wedding photo shown here looks spectacular on the gold and black background. Don't be afraid of uising color and patterned papers in your album.

Using Patterned Papers

When putting together any scrapbook, patterned background papers can express the emotions in the photos included on a page. It isn't much different for heritage photos.

Consider the feeling a photo presents to the viewer when choosing backgrounds for the album pages.

Many patterned papers are available both to be used as the entire background and as coordinating mats. Generally, the small, repeat patterns such as dots, narrow stripes, small checks and plaids are perfect for matting photos. They add life to the page without overpowering the images or the page itself. The page at the left features denim and burlap mats to reinforce the country theme of the photo. A good rule of thumb is to first mat the photo with a solid paper, then add a second, patterned mat behind it.

When choosing patterned papers, be sure they enhance and reinforce the mood of the photo. A funky, playful pattern is inappropriate for a formal family portrait, yet could work well with a black and white photo of a child engaged in a fun activity.

Tools

There are numerous tools designed especially for creating unique memory albums and scrapbooks. Those used in creating a heritage album can be as varied as the times depicted on the pages. As with color and patterns of papers used, consider the mood of each photo as you're choosing which scissors to use when trimming the design elements and which punches, stickers or Punch-Outs™ you'll use.

When using tools on heritage pages, remember to maintain the dignity and integrity of the photos throughout. Use the appropriate tools, enhancing the photos with elements which help tell the story depicted on each page. Some examples could be deckle scissors, fleur-de-lis punches and decorative and round corner cutters.

Ensign Don Choate 1960

Scissors & Cutting Tools

Of course straight-edged scissors are necessary when creating any album, especially a heritage album. To achieve the perfect straight edges with little effort, a personal trimmer is excellent. The sliding blade style is more accurate than the guillotine type. It has the ability to shave very narrow edges off paper mats and photos and is available in a size to accommodate 8½"x11" sheets of paper.

In addition to straight edges, decorative edges enhance mats or the borders on pages. There are literally dozens of styles of pattern-edged scissors which cut a particular decorative edge on paper. Several styles are very appropriate in creating a heritage album, including Victorian or romantic styles and especially the deckle-edge. It very nicely recreates those uneven edges found on old photographs.

When using decorative scissors, remember to evaluate whether they will enhance or detract from the overall look and feel of the page. Save the modern style or jagged scissors for later photos and layouts.

Corner edgers are scissors which are used just to cut the corners off photos, mats and pages. They add wonderful touches to pages, but can be tricky to use;

Once the album page is finished and ready to go into the album, a sheet protector is the safest place for it to be stored within the album. However, the sleeve must be PVC-free (polyvinyl chloride free). Look for page protectors made from polyester (Mylar brand), polypropylene or polyethylene; their packaging will be labeled "photo-safe" or "archival". These products are chemically stable for encasing your photographs.

Deloris
Christiansen
Christmas
1955 & 1950

make sure the paper corner fits snugly in the tool before cutting.

Other cutting tools available include circle and oval cutters, which make perfect circles and ovals in a snap. If you'd rather not invest in those specialty cutters, use templates and trace the shapes onto mats or photos, then cut out the shapes with scissors.

Punch-Outs™, Stickers & Die Cuts

Punch-Outs™, stickers and die-cuts are used in similar ways on pages. They can transform a boring album page into one which is exciting to view, adding clever elements to it.

Punch-Outs™ are printed paper elements, punched from a book and used to enhance album pages, generally reinforcing a theme, such as the pansies on the page at the right. Punch-Outs™ are also used to create borders on pages and to decorate the areas around photos. They differ from die-cuts in that they are drawn and enhanced art, not simply plain paper cut into shapes. They were especially designed for scrapbooking and offer the ease of being pre-matted—all you do is punch and glue. Because of the number of Punch-Outs™ in each book, they're a great value.

Stickers, such as those shown on the page at the left, are adhesive-backed and, though less economical than Punch-Outs™, can be colorful additions to album pages, especially when they contribute to the theme or feeling of the page. Stickers can be found in many different themes and styles, from the very plain, small images to larger, more elaborate pieces.

Although less detailed, die-cuts are also used to reinforce the action or theme of an album page. Die-cuts are available in numerous shapes and are glued to the page around the photos. They are cut from plain or patterned papers, then enhanced with pens to complete the image or used as a base for journaling. The star on the page at the right does a terrific job of carrying the military theme through the page.

Punches

Paper punches are available in many styles and are used to embellish everyday scrapbooks. While many are inappropriate for use with formal heritage portraits, there are some which work well in a heritage album. And, because the album does include modern photos documenting today's generations, those less formal punches can be used on the appropriate pages.

A corner slot punch (used as shown at left) is nice to have when making heritage pages. It allows you to easily mount your photos as a non-permanent mounting technique. You simply slip the corners of the mat securely into the tool and punch. The resulting slots easily accomodate the corners of your photo, keeping it in place while allowing you to remove it at any time.

Corner punches are used to decoratively punch the corners of mats and photos, allowing the paper underneath to show through the punched holes. When used, they provide distinctive and customized looks to the pages. Edge punches accomplish the same effect along the edges of mats and paper embellishments.

Pens

Pen work around photos and journaling near them add personality to all scrapbook pages. The pens should be acid-free permanent-ink pens. Ball point, water-based pens are not permanent, can bleed and may damage the photos. There are many photo-safe pens available in dozens of colors and in several tip sizes.

When we consider heritage albums, we think of using only black ink, but gold (used on the page at the left) and silver, along with dark colors, enhance the formal colors found in older photos. If you're unsure about writing directly on the photo, write on the mat or on the background paper. Or journal on a separate paper, cut it out, then glue it near the photo.

Adhesives

Archivists and conservationists encourage people who are creating their heritage albums to use non-permanent means of affixing photos to pages. This makes it eas-

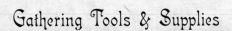

ier to remove the photos for sharing, duplicating and restoring, should that be necessary. To avoid using adhesives directly on the photo, use photo corners to mount them onto mats or backgrounds.

Photo mounts are an excellent option; they are double-sided adhesive squares or strips. The mounts are placed on the back of the photo or mat, then it's positioned onto the page and pressed in place. Should the mat need to be removed for any reason, an adhesive neutralizer can be used on the photo mount. The other option is xylene-free glue. This glue will not harm the photos themselves, yet will permanently attach the elements together.

Album Organization

Once the photos have been gathered from various sources, organized and stored in a safe environment, and the tools to be used have been determined and gathered, the next step is determining how you want to organize the album itself.

Whether you have many pictures of your ancestors and assorted relatives or only a few, creating a chronological scrapbook can easily present your family's history. With each page bringing a new face of the family, this album lets you see parents, grandparents and distant ancestors within a very logical sequence. A chronological album may be arranged to take the viewer from the present to the past or from past to present. Generally, it's easiest to work from present to past, since the starting point is definitive and the album is easily added to as more distant ancestors are discovered.

Instead of a single album, you may choose to make two such albums: One of your mother's lineage and one of your father's.

For those with very few photos of ancestors, a "Time Line" layout is a unique and very informative account of your heritage. This type of album is organized by historical periods during which ancestral photos were taken. Research the year or decade each photo was taken and journal about what was going on then. Paired with just one photo, the sense and feeling of the era is depicted for future generations to experience and appreciate.

In addition, add color-copies (using acid-free paper) of old magazine photos showing activities or events your family experienced and arrange them among your photos. Journal how the activities affected your family, their memories, and the changes caused by the historical events of the times. The page shown here is an example of this technique which gives a feeling of the era depicted in the photograph.

In addition to the old-fashioned photo corners available years ago, we now have at our disposal many types of decorative corners, all found in the scrapbooking section of many stores.

The Basics
of Scrapbooking

All your hard work of rescuing and collecting photos, reproducing them, then gathering all the tools and materials is done and now you're ready to actually construct the album pages. You will find many useful examples and ideas in this section for making beautiful album pages. Your heritage album, filled with all the nostalgic photos and sentimental stories you've gathered, will become a wonderful and precious keepsake to be handed down through your family.

To ensure the longevity of your heritage album, you'll want to take care to store it in the best environment possible. As with the photos you rescued when you first began, the finished album must be stored in a similar, safe environment. The environment you enjoy best is also best to extend the life of your album. Your living room is the perfect place. Avoid extremes in temperature and humidity. Humid atmospheres such as in basements, attics or near outer, uninsulated walls of a house can encourage mold growth on the photos.

When displaying albums, avoid prolonged exposure to light on the photos. Protect them from direct handling; sheet protectors eliminate that possibility as the album is passed from relative to relative. The sleeves also eliminate the possibility of scratches on the photos or of the photo surfaces rubbing together.

We're not sure heritage albums are ever really "finished." Once started, the process of collecting and discovering photos and stories of ancestors and family members may take on a life of its own. And you may become the family historian.

Your album was made for enjoyment—both in its construction and in the pleasure of viewing the finished results. Share it with friends and family, secure in the knowledge that you've rescued a part of your heritage. Having used the protective measures outlined in this book, both during construction and afterwards, you can be assured the album will last through future generations.

Cropping Photos

Trimming a photo to a certain size or shape is called "cropping." The cropped photo should work within the layout of a page. Not all photos should be cropped—especially when dealing with heritage photos. Cropping photos can add exciting elements to album pages; just be sure you're comfortable with cutting the photographs before beginning. If not, color copy the photos onto acid-free paper and use the copies in the album.

When cropping photos, be sure to leave historical items such as houses or cars in the picture. Trim away the extraneous areas such as sky or ground to bring the focal area of the photo closer. Use a plastic template for smooth ovals and perfect circles. Place the template on top of the photo and draw the shape on the photo with an acid-free photo pencil. Then cut inside the line.

Silhouetting is cutting around the person or object. This allows the focal point of the photo to become very important on the album page. Before using this technique on one-of-a-kind heritage photos, color copy them and cut the copies for the album. Cut along the edge of the focal area, removing all the background.

Bumping out one section of a photo is silhouetting one area, while leaving the rest of the photo with a background. Again, because this technique is radical, be sure to copy your valuable heritage photos and cut the copies.

Color Polaroid photos cannot be cropped. With these photos, it's best to cut a square framing mat slightly larger than the Polaroid photo and then cut an oval, circle or square opening in the center to lay over the photo allowing the person to be seen through the inner frame opening. Black & white Polaroid photos, however, can be cropped with no adverse effects. This is due to the differences in how each type of Polaroid film is made and developed.

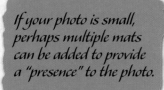

If your photo is small, perhaps multiple mats can be added to provide a "presence" to the photo.

Matting Photos

You probably already know the golden rule of scrapbooking with patterned papers: Mat the photos with plain paper! Adding a mat to photos gives them more of a presence by framing them and separating the photos from the background paper. When surrounded by a mat, photos do not compete with the background papers, but are enhanced by them.

To soften edges and corners of squares and rectangles, so prevalent when working with heritage photos, there are several matting options. The edges can be covered with laser-cut lace paper, as is shown on the page at the right, or wavy borders can be added to the page to draw the eye away from the sharp corners. Using pattern-edged scissors on mats around the photos will also soften the edges. Just adding an oval or circular mat around the photo without cutting the photo itself could be the solution needed.

To mat the photos, adhere the cropped photo to a sheet of paper and cut ⅛"-½" away, forming a mat. Use plain or patterned paper for the mat and straight-edged or decorative edge scissors to cut it. When matting a photo which has been cut into a silhouette or bumped out, it's best to use plain paper for the mat and to keep it narrow.

Adding multiple mats draws attention to the photo and varying the sizes of the mats adds interest. Mixing mat shapes, as was done on Robert's page, adds excitement to a layout and makes the photo the star of the page. For drama on an album page, mat an oval photo first with a slightly larger oval mat, then again with a rectangular shape.

If you are adhering to the archivists' method of keeping everything removable, use photo corners to mount the pictures to the background mat. Or, place a traditional photo mat over the picture; glue three edges onto the album page, then slip the photo behind the mat under the unglued fourth edge. However, be aware that the photos will shift as the pages are turned.

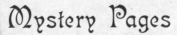

Mystery Pages

Chances are, you'll come across at least a few ancestral photos that just can't be identified. Instead of leaving them out, create pages using these mystery photos, then compile them into one album. On the back of each, write what is known about the person or maybe where the photo was found and the approximate year it was taken. Then take your "Mystery Album" to family gatherings or reunions and ask if anyone knows anything about the photos.

Leaving one mat larger than the others can provide an area for journaling around the photo, as shown on Robert's page, above.

When you get the information, add it to the page in a journaled form, then insert the page at the proper place in your heritage album.

Layout

Continuity and perspective play major roles in the layout of album pages. Choose photos that closely relate to each other, whether by actual family relationship to each other, in the action portrayed or in the time depicted by the photos. This provides continuity to the layout, tying the elements together.

The size of the design elements has a big impact on heritage album pages. A small photo can be overwhelmed with too many large embellishments. And any thought to conveying emotion through patterns and color can be covered up by a very large photo. If you have only one or two small photos to showcase on a page, and have stories or information to include, journaling can be added around the photo (see the pages at left).

If you have a large photo and wish to add journaling, or have many photos of one event or person, a double-page spread can be very effective. The photos are arranged on two pages, and similar, coordinating backgrounds, colors and enhancements are used. The freedom of the extra space adds more options, and the pages are very striking when viewed in an album (see the example below).

In developing the layout of a page, first pull the elements together. This includes photos, journaled stories and any memorabilia. Consider the colors in these pieces and the era in which they existed. Using this information, select your background paper first, then decide how the pieces will be matted and mounted. Make sure the colors and textures all work together, then temporarily place them on the page. Move the elements around until they're placed most effectively for telling your story—overlapping the photos and other elements is fine! Crop, mat and affix the pieces to the page.

Vary the sizes of the photos, if possible. A variety of sizes can create a focal point and add impact to the layout design. One larger photo on a page establishes the theme or subject of the page with the smaller photos and blocks of journaling reinforcing it and telling the story.

Most often, heritage photos are nearly the same size, but to add variety and interest to the pages, a photocopier can be used to enlarge some photos.

Journaling

While the photos in a heritage album are "the stars", the journaled stories tie everything together. They bring personality to photos, allowing glimpses into past lives. If you have access to a computer, that's certainly the easiest method of journaling and the variety of fonts now available can provide added feeling to the pages. Simply type the stories, print them, then crop, mat and add them to each album page around or near the photos.

Hand journaling adds a human touch to the pages, but as the writer simplifies the text to make it easier to hand-journal some details may be lost. Because this album is a record of your family, the more stories you can discover and include, the more complete will be the album. Don't worry about including too much! As the album is passed among family members, all of it will be read—and may spark more, related stories. There are many writing styles to be used in hand-journaling, but your own handwriting adds a part of you to the album.

When writing the text that will accompany a photo, don't forget all the details. Be sure to include who, when, where, what and why—at least as much as you know. Then elaborate with as many details as you can remember or discover about the photo or the person depicted. Don't worry that you may be writing too much; any and all information will be greatly appreciated by everyone who reads the journaled pieces.

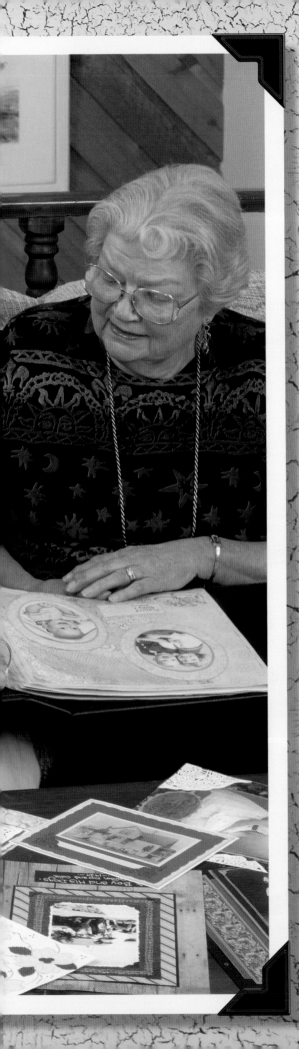

Bringing It All Together

A heritage album does not need to be page after page of black backgrounds with square and rectangular photos arranged in rows. Exciting pages can be developed around those old photographs using patterned backgrounds with colored mats and accents. Even though the majority of the photos are black and white or sepia tones, an abundance of color can be brought into the page layouts to compliment those photos. The addition of colors and patterns enriches the layouts while enhancing the shading and textures within the photographs.

Within this section, we've provided some techniques for creating unique album pages using old photographs. Many times you'll have one or two photos for a page; the challenge then becomes how to fill the page to support the photos—you'll find some answers in this chapter. The supplies we used are listed near each album page example. You'll see the names of the scissors or embellishments used, as well as the books where the background papers are found—if it says "(new)", it's a paper from this book.

Adding texture to heritage page layouts can be done a variety of ways. Whether it's with paper strips woven into a pattern for a customized handmade look or paper doilies under the photos for an elegant feel, the techniques reinforce the feelings of the photographs. If you have a keepsake ribbon, we've included an idea for using it on page 45. And the examples of pen work we've included are quite simple though very effective, adding elegance to the pages.

Your heritage album will be a one-of-a-kind treasure, featuring your photos and memorabilia in creative layouts. Some pages may be elegant, some charming, many sentimental, but all will be irreplaceable family heirlooms carrying your family's ancestry packed with all the care you will have put into their creation.

Paper Strips

The formal, refined personality of Grandfather Grindal is very well conveyed with the use of these patterned papers. But we also see the playful side of him as he relaxes in the park with his dog behind him. The woven strips at the corners imply how he lived his life; orderly yet peppered with joviality. Glue three ¼" wide strips across the top and bottom of the page, leaving the corner 1¼" loose. Weave three ¼" strips through the loose ends of the longer strips and glue all in place.

Paper Pizazz™: brown swirl, brown suede (Black & White Photos)
Solid Paper Pizazz™: dark brown (Solid Muted Colors)
Gold pen: Milky Gel Roller by Marvy®
Page designer: Katie Hacker for Hot Off The Press

Choose which patterned paper to use by pulling the theme from the photo as with this sandstone paper and beach picture. While Frank Park scouts the area, the paper strips echo the directions of a compass—bet he wished he'd had one here! This photo was kept intact with the mat board it had been previously placed on in 1930. Rather than risk causing damage by removing it, the mat and photo were color-copied onto acid-free paper. The copy is secured to the page with photo corners, while the original is stored separately—great archiving techniques!

Paper Pizazz™: sandstone (Textured Papers), brown suede (Black & White Photos), handmade oatmeal (Handmade Papers)
Solid Paper Pizazz™: black (Solid Jewel Tones)
Decorative scissors: deckle by Family Treasures™
Black pen: Zig® Writer by EK Success Ltd.
Page designer: Katie Hacker for Hot Off The Press

Paper strips make an easy page border. They frame the page nicely and offer room to journal along. ½" wide strips are used here with cut outs to embellish them. This is a great page that spans generations with the mother and sister at top and, thirty years later, their daughters (at the bottom) engaged in the same activity. Combining the two photos in one page design does a great job of showing the continuity of families and proves that all things do come full circle.

Paper Pizazz™: blue & pink plaid, white stitching on pink *(new)*
Solid Paper Pizazz™: dark blue, dusty light blue *(Solid Muted Colors)*
Cut outs: flower corners and blossoms *(Embellishments)*
Decorative scissors: deckle by Family Treasures™
Black pen: Zig® Writer by EK Success Ltd.
Page designer: Katie Hacker for Hot Off The Press

Stickers are a fast simple way to border a page or embellish a journaled area. Many sticker images work well with heritage photos. Tint an area of the photo with a colored pencil for an added element of fun, then pick up that color in the patterned and plain papers!

Paper Pizazz™: pink embossed roses, pink & blue plaid *(new)*
Solid Paper Pizazz™: salmon, white *(Plain Pastels)*
Flowers, purse, doll, jump rope stickers: by The Gifted Line
Decorative scissors: deckle by Family Treasures™
Red pencil: Memory Pencils by EK Success Ltd.
Black pen: Zig® Writer by EK Success Ltd.
Page designer: Katie Hacker for Hot Off The Press

Multiple Page Spreads

This two page spread technique makes a great companion page. The portraits were matted using the same two sheets of patterned paper. Cut an 8½"x6¼" rectangle from each patterned paper. Carefully cut out a 7¾"x5" center. After you mat the photos on the solid black paper (trimming with pattern scissors), mat them once on the smaller rectangle then again on the larger sheet. Mat the whole piece on black then again on jewel green.

Paper Pizazz™: green suede, white stripe on green (new)
Solid Paper Pizazz™: green, black (Solid Jewel Tones)
Rub-ons: Magic Memories™ by True Expressions™
Decorative scissors: colonial by Fiskars®
Page designer: LeNae Gerig for Hot Off The Press

Each element in the three page spread below coordinates to showcase three generations of this family branch. The background papers are of the same pattern and texture implying a strong relationship in the pages, the matting and journaling technique remains similar throughout and the tripple corner strips hint at how many pages are in the series. Carrying over each of these elements tie the pages as tightly as the love that binds the family.

Paper Pizazz™: green suede, burgundy suede, brown suede (new)
Solid Paper Pizazz™: black, green, burgundy (Solid Jewel Tones)
Photo corners: copper by Canson
Decorative scissors: deckle by Family Treasures™
Black pen: Zig® Scroll and Brush pen by E.K. Success, Ltd.
Page designer: Katie Hacker for Hot Off The Press

Create a multiple page spread by using similar elements on each page. One piece of patterned paper can be cut into two 5½"x8½" rectangles—one for each page of each spread, then mat each on black paper. Glue to the center of brown plain paper. Affix the photos to black mats with gold photo corners, then glue the mats to the patterned paper. Draw a — • — border around the large black mats. Journal below the photos, and on the brown paper. Use a third patterned paper to make eight triangles. Arrange the elements as shown, glue to the background paper, and affix a triangle to the outside corners of each spread.

Paper Pizazz™: peach stripe, argyle peach, orange & brown checks (new)

Solid Paper Pizazz™: black, brown (Solid Jewel Tones)

Photo corners: gold by Canson

Page designer: Katie Hacker for Hot Off The Press

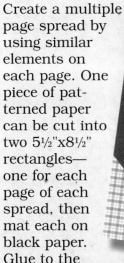

Pen Work

Embellishing your page design with pen work is an opportunity to be creative and artistic. Some of the best pen work we've seen is the free-flowing form of what comes from the heart. These little holly leaves are simply a series of "waves" linked with a free-form loopy line. Groups of three red dots resemble holly berries while the white dots look like snow flakes. This photo isn't cropped; the green strip that has the pen work on it was trimmed on one side with pattern-edged scissors and laid over the excess area of the photo.

Paper Pizazz™: green marble *(Pretty Papers)*, burgundy handmade *(Handmade Papers)*, gold *(Metallic Papers)*
Solid Paper Pizazz™: black, hunter green *(Solid Jewel Tones)*
Decorative scissors: jumbo classic wave by Family Treasures™
Gold, red and silver pens: Gel Roller by Marvy®
Page designer: LeNae Gerig for Hot Off The Press

Wide mats are perfect for pen embellishments. A few lines, squiggles and dots convey the festivities portrayed in these photos. Pattern-edged scissors can echo the natural deckled edge of many heritage photos, and when used on a mat, coordinates the page. Rub-on embellishments give the look and texture of a rubber stamp quickly and easily to celebrate the history of this family.

Paper Pizazz™: burgundy stripe *(new)*, gold *(Metallic Papers)*
Solid Paper Pizazz™: red *(Plain Brights)*
Gold rub-ons: leaves, embellishments and numbers by Magic Memory
Decorative scissors: deckle by Family Treasures™
Black pen: Zig® Writer by EK Success, Ltd.
Page designer: Katie Hacker for Hot Off The Press

Creating detailed pen work is a great way to fill space when you only have one photo to showcase. A large, elaborate mat combines colors and patterns that speak of all the things that little girls are made of. What fun the variety of mat shapes add to this page design! Use the red pen to draw random circles on the background paper adding white highlights to each. Use the green pen to draw stems and leaves on each and to coil spirals here and there. White tri-dots and a bit of journaling offer the finishing touches.

Paper Pizazz™: red & white checked (new), cherries on black (Sweet Companions)
Solid Paper Pizazz™: black (Solid Jewel Tones), white (Plain Pastels)
Red, green and white pens: Milky Gel Roller by Marvy®
Decorative scissors: scallop by Fiskars®
Page designer: LeNae Gerig for Hot Off The Press

Elaborate, fancy pen work is easy to do with stencils! Mat a photo on a large mat with plenty of space all around. Place a stencil for the first initial in the upper corner and tape it in place while you work with a pen to fill it in. This photo was cut away where the two overlapped, though the integrity of the photo remains unharmed. Stenciled fleur-de-lis embellishments add interest to the page, while photo corners on the mat add elegance. Choosing the embossed daisies background paper ties the page together as it echoes the sense of texture provided by the stenciled pen work.

Paper Pizazz™: embossed pink daisies, burgundy moiré (new)
Alphabet stencil: Monogram Magic™ by Delta
Photo corners: gold by Canson
Gold pen: Milky Gel Roller by Marvy®
Page designer: Katie Hacker for Hot Off The Press

Bordering a Page

Adding a border to your heritage page offers a number of simple, elegant looks. This formal portrait carries such a sense of reverence for this family's father that's implied with the "royal" looking punches used around the border. Save the punched-out shapes to glue around the mat to carry the element throughout the page. Punch a few shapes from the contrasting paper color to create interest and coordination within the design.

Paper Pizazz™: green moiré, white dot on navy *(new)*
Solid Paper Pizazz™: maroon, black *(Solid Jewel Tones)*
Border punch: McGill, Inc.
Decorative scissors: Victorian by Fiskars®
White pen: Milky Gel Roller by Marvy®
Page designer: LeNae Gerig for Hot Off The Press

Punch-Outs™ are a wonderfully quick and easy way to get elaborate art elements onto your page. Use border and corner Punch-Out™ images to frame your page, leading the eye around the photo layout design. Flower and lace images are perfect for childhood photos. Choose colors that play on the personalities of the family members shown in the photos and embellishments that coordinate well with them.

Paper Pizazz™: pink embossed roses *(new)*, gold *(Metallic Papers)*
Solid Paper Pizazz™: mauve *(Solid Muted Colors)*, ivory *(Solid Pastels)*
Punch-Outs™: "Memories" on lace *(Tops & Bottoms)*
Cut outs: dried flowers *(Embellishments)*
Gold pen: Hybrid Gel Roller by Marvy®
Page designer: Katie Hacker for Hot Off The Press

Paper Doilies & Laser Lace

Laser-cut lace never looked so festive! It's a great paper to use for wedding photos. Cut out and mat two pieces of lace paper onto yellow. Arrange them diagonally on the upper right and lower left corners, trim and use the excess to frame the other two corners. It's okay to use a more festive scissor edge on fun heritage photos like this. Journaling around a circle mat gives an opportunity to really interact with the page, too!

Paper Pizazz™: white daisies *(Floral Papers)*, laser lace *(Romantic Papers)*
Solid Paper Pizazz™: yellow *(Solid Muted Colors)*, white *(Plain Pastels)*, green *(Solid Jewel Tones)*
Decorative scissors: ripply by McGill, Inc.
Green pen: Zig® Writer by EK Success, Ltd.
Page designer: Katie Hacker for Hot Off The Press

Childhood heritage photos can offer a great opportunity to be creative and have fun with your page designs. This bold layout intersects lines, colors, plaids and frills all in the name of a child—and it works quite well! Mat a square doily and glue it diagonally to a pink and yellow plaid paper. Use a second doily to make corners all around and embellish each with a rose sticker. These scissor edges echo the doily edge and coordinate nicely when used on the journal mat.

Paper Pizazz™: pink & yellow plaid *(new)*
Solid Paper Pizazz™: yellow, pink *(Plain Pastels)*
White roses stickers: ©Mrs. Grossman's Paper Company
Doily: 8"x8" white by Artifacts, Inc.
Adhesive: sticky dots by Therm O Web (or simply use acid-free glue)
Decorative scissors: jumbo lace scallop by Family Treasures™
White pen: Milky Gel Roller by Marvy®
Page designer: LeNae Gerig for Hot Off The Press

Journaling

Computers offer a wonderful way to journal easily. Choose a font with a matching appearance to your page, whether whimsical or antique. Be sure to use acid-free and lignin-free paper in your printer to include it in your album. Overlap the elements to keep the eye moving, and use paper strips along opposing corners to lead the eye onto the page.

Paper Pizazz™: antique lace *(Very Pretty Papers)*, gold *(Metallic Papers)*
Solid Paper Pizazz™: burgundy *(Solid Jewel Tones)*, ivory *(Plain Pastels)*
Decorative scissors: deckle by Family Treasures™
Page designer: Katie Hacker for Hot Off The Press

Journaling on the left hand page of a two page spread makes a great companion page—and could serve as an introduction to an album section of that branch of the family. Remove the center oval of one pattern paper and mat the remainder onto white creating a large area for journaling. Crop the photo into an oval and mat onto the pattern paper oval. Glue to another patterned sheet and journal in the white oval area.

Paper Pizazz™: embossed black roses, black satin *(new)*
Solid Paper Pizazz™: white *(Plain Pastels)*
Punch-Outs™: letters *(Pretty ABC's)*
Decorative scissors: wave by Family Treasures™
Black pen: Zig® Writer by EK Success Ltd.
Page designer: Katie Hacker for Hot Off The Press

Journaling favorite sayings of a relative is a wonderfully personal way to remember an ancestor in your heritage album. Whether it's a list of favorite quotes, hobbies, or anecdotes they've passed through the family, this page of historical ancestry will be a treasure for years to come. Use a computer to type the words. Print it on archival quality paper, then mat it on coordinating paper. Affix it to the page along with a photo of the relative for a page that will carry family memories for future generations to enjoy.

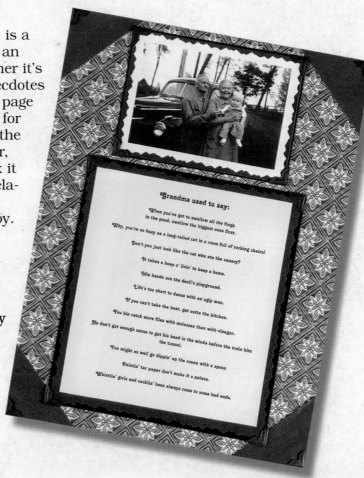

Paper Pizazz™: fancy black tiles (new)
Solid Paper Pizazz™: cream, black, brown
    (Solid Jewel Tones)
Photo corners: black by Canson
Decorative scissors: deckle wave by Family
    Treasures™
Page designer: Katie Hacker for Hot Off
    The Press

Allow your journaling to be deeply personal, as is this example. The memories your words bring out will be priceless as the years pass. Those who read your words in the years that come will have such an insight into their own heritage. Breaking the story up into separate journal boxes offers freedom in layout design and provides elements to fill any empty spaces.

Paper Pizazz™: mint plaid (Pastel Plaids),
    laser lace (Romantic Papers)
Solid Paper Pizazz™: pink, mint (Plain
    Pastels)
Punch-Outs™: flower corners (Sweet
    Companions)
Decorative scissors: mini Victorian ele-
    gance by Family Treasures™
Page designer: Katie Hacker for Hot Off
    The Press

Texture with Rubber Stamps

Even a novice stamper can create this lovely background with rubber stamps! The contrasting colors of gold and black bring out all the gorgeous tones in black and white photos. Randomly stamp the ivy onto black paper. Press the stamp into the gold ink and turn it's position after each imprint. Be sure to let the ink dry before you affix the mat. Copper photo corners enhance the antique appearance of this page and the crackle patterned paper echoes the age of the era.

Paper Pizazz™: crackle *(Textured Papers)*, gold *(Metallic Papers)*
Solid Paper Pizazz™: black *(Solid Jewel Tones)*
Ivy leaf rubber stamp: Great Impressions©
Photo corners: gold by Canson
Decorative scissors: mini antique Victorian by Family Treasures™
Black pen: Zig® Writer by EK Success, Ltd.
Page designer: LeNae Gerig for Hot Off The Press

Stamp each image onto plain paper and cut out to make a "mask". Stamp the baby shoes, let dry and lay the shoe mask over the image. Then stamp the flowers to overlap the mask. The area of the image that overlaps the mask will not appear on the page. Use this technique to stamp the layered daisy heads, also. Stamp the mat paper before matting the photos. After trimming the edges, lightly apply cocoa ink to the edges with a makeup sponge for an antique appearance.

Paper Pizazz™: lace *(Pretty Papers)*
Solid Paper Pizazz™: peach *(Solid Pastels)*
Cardstock: clay brown by DMD Industries
Shasta daisy, baby shoes, baby's breath rubber stamps: by Stampendous
Gold metallic pigment ink: Top Boss by Clearsnap
Copper embossing powder: by Stampendous
Pigment ink pads: cocoa by Colorbox, amber by Clearsnap
Copper pen: Metallic Roller by Zebra
Decorative scissors: ripple by Fiskars®
Page Designer: Linda Ipple

Rubber stamps aren't limited to being used on plain papers only. These stamps enhance the patterned paper behind them, adding to rather than competing with the design of the page. Begin with two gold pen lines to border the page and draw random squiggles to embellish the inner line. Then stamp the image in the upper right and lower left corners, using embossing tools to create a glistening shine. Emboss the edges of one photo's mat, and emboss the journal area with the date. Notice how the letters patterned paper helps to tell the story of this woman going to school away from home.

Paper Pizazz™: tapestry *(Very Pretty Papers)*, letters *(For Black & White Photos)*
Cardstock: sage, burgundy, parchment by DMD Industries
Ivy leaves rubber stamp: by Rubberstampede
Embossing ink: Top Boss by Clearsnap
Embossing powder: copper by Stampendous
Decorative scissors: deckle by Fiskars®
Copper pen: Metallic Roller Pen by Zebra
Embossing pens: Writer™ and Calligraphy™ by EK Success, Ltd.
Page designer: Linda Ippel

These gold stamps in each corner offer an elegant framed appearance. The drawn "S" curves in each corner of the mat pulls the eye into the photo. The burgundy suede mat paper offers a sense of tenderness to this heritage moment. Outlining each element with a gold pen gives a gold leafing effect of antiquity.

Paper Pizazz™: burgundy dashed, burgundy suede *(new)*
Solid Paper Pizazz™: black *(Solid Jewel Tones)*
Illuminated corner rubber stamp: by Rubberstampede
Gold embossing ink: Top Boss by Clearsnap
Embossing powder: by Stampendous
Gold paint pen: Metallic Calligraphy by Marvy®
Gold pen: Metallic Roller Pen by Zebra
Decorative scissors: deckle by Fiskars®
Page designer: Linda Ippel

Texture with Embossing Stencils

.Tokyo. 1937. Mizuno Family.

The subtle texture of embossed hearts is a perfect touch to convey the love shared in these three generations of Japanese women. Embossing stencils are easiest to use if you have a light source behind the paper, such as a window or light box. Rub over the paper with a round stylus, pressing firmly into the corners. The image will be raised on the opposite side of the paper, so work on the back of the paper in order to have the raised image on the front.

Paper Pizazz™: burgundy roses *(new)*
Solid Paper Pizazz™: black *(Solid Jewel Tones)*
Cardstock: 12"x12" white by DMD Industries
Brass stencil: American Traditional Stencil
Decorative scissors: deckle and imperial by Fiskars®
Black pen: Zig® Millenium by EK Success Ltd.
Page designer: LeNae Gerig for Hot Off The Press

With so many shapes and designs, it's easy to find an image that'll work with your heritage photos. Use acid-free colored pencils to touch up black and white photos for a fun addition to children's photos. Notice the papers are colors found in the photos, too.

Paper Pizazz™: peach argyle, peach & pink checks *(Pastel Plaid Papers)*
Solid Paper Pizazz™: blue *(Plain Brights)*, ivory *(Solid Pastel Papers)*
Stencil: Emboss Art by McGill, Inc.
Decorative scissors: deckle by Fiskars®
Red, blue, yellow pencils: Memory Pencils by EK Success Ltd.
Page designer: LeNae Gerig for Hot Off The Press

Betty Jean and Billy
1945

Aunt Betty Jean and Uncle Billy Roy Warren were only a year apart and very tight friends. Five years later my mother Judy was born into the family. Betty Jean and Billy had done everything together for so many years they didn't know how they were ever going to include a third person. They didn't know what role they were suddenly supposed to play! Uncle Billy had wanted a baby boy. Aunt B.J. just wished the new baby wasn't going to be so young! Those two stayed tight as knit woolen sweaters for many years; they always got into mischief together and were always being told to 'include your baby sister, Judy!' They didn't always remember. But when they did, mom says they always had a lot of fun!

Torn Paper Texture

All the elements on this page work to soften the rectangular edges of the photo eliminating the need to crop—a great technique for irreplaceable heritage photos that you just can't cut. The torn paper mats soften the photo's hard edges, while the overlapped strips in the corners keep the focus on the photo. The rounded, embossed gold numerals in the Punch-Outs™ echo the formality of the photo while the ferns and white daisies papers imply the feminine personality of this young woman.

Paper Pizazz™: green ferns *(new)*, white daisies *(Floral Papers)*
Solid Paper Pizazz™: hunter green *(Solid Jewel Tones)*
Punch-Outs™: numbers *(Pretty ABC Punch-Outs™)*
Gold pen: Milky Gel Roller by Marvy®
Page designer: Katie Hacker for Hot Off The Press

This page is a perfect example of letting colored and patterned papers echo the words of your family's story. More than just the photo tell us that these were down-to-earth, good folks. With a bit of the car and part of the yard and house, it'd be a shame to crop this shot, so the edges were softened and texture was provided by using rich patterned papers and torn edges. The off-set handmade green paper mat adds interest and keeps the eye moving around the page.

Paper Pizazz™: cedar handmade, handmade green, handmade oatmeal *(Handmade Papers)*
Solid Paper Pizazz™: brown *(Solid Muted Colors)*
Gold pen: Milky Gel Roller by Marvy®
Page designer: Katie Hacker for Hot Off The Press

12"x12" Pages from 8½"x11" Papers

Patterned papers can do a terrific job of helping you journal! A famous attribute of Europe is their cobblestone roadways—this paper echoes that characteristic perfectly. Mat the cobblestone paper onto oatmeal paper and cut a ½" edge with patterned scissors. Mount in the center of the 12"x12" brown handmade-look paper and arrange your matted photos overlapping the cobblestone paper.

Paper Pizazz™: cobblestone *(Textured Papers)*, handmade oatmeal, brown handmade *(The Handmade Look)*
Solid Paper Pizazz™: maroon, blue *(Solid Jewel Tones)*
Decorative scissors: deckle and deckle wave by Family Treasures™
Black pen: Zig® Writer by EK Success, Ltd.
Page designer: Katie Hacker for Hot Off The Press

Ernestine Traveling in Europe before the war

All the elements on this page enhance the sepia tone photos shown. The metallic gold background paper echoes the flash of the boys' sports jackets, the brick paper carries forth the brick of the high school building pictured behind them, and the circles, made to look like basketballs, show what sport they played. The copper photo corners and mats really help bring out the photo's shading.

Paper Pizazz™: brick wall *(Textured Papers)*, gold, copper *(Heavy Metal Papers)*
Solid Paper Pizazz™: black *(Solid Jewel Tones)*
Photo corners: copper by Canson
Gold pen: Milky Gel Roller by Marvy®
Page designer: LeNae Gerig for Hot Off The Press

Gordon Gettes, S.D. High School 1940

Patterned papers can really convey the fun times of an era as does this paper for the 1950's! Measure in 5" from two opposite corners of the 8½"x11" record paper, draw a diagonal line intersecting through this point and cut along it to make two triangles; glue to a sheet of blue 12"x12" paper. Triple mat a large photo on black, red and pin-stripe blue paper. Journal your memories of the day, mat similarly and place on the page as shown. Cut records from the remaining paper and use to embellish the empty space between the triangles.

Paper Pizazz™: 45 records *(1950's &60's Papers)*, navy pin stripe *(new)*
Solid Paper Pizazz™: red, blue *(Solid Bright Papers)*, black *(Solid Jewel Tones)*
Musical note punch: Marvy®
Decorative scissors: deckle by Family Treasures™
Page designer: LeNae Gerig for Hot Off The Press

Ribbon can provide rich texture to many heritage page layouts. A keepsake ribbon from an old dress or special occasion can be washed and dried, then sprayed with an acid-buffer (available in most craft stores) to be included in the album. Notice how patterned edged scissors and the overlapped photos helps to soften the hard edges and angular shapes of the page. Cut two sheets of laser lace to elegantly border an 8½"x11" patterned paper on a 12"x12" page.

Paper Pizazz™: tapestry *(Pretty Papers)*, burgundy moiré *(new)*, lace *(Romantic Papers)*
Solid Paper Pizazz™: green, burgundy *(Solid Jewel Tones)*, ivory *(Plain Pastels)*
White ribbon: by Offray & Son, Inc.
Decorative scissors: Victorian by Family Treasures™
Black pen: Zig® Writer by EK Success, Ltd.
Page designer: Katie Hacker for Hot Off The Press

Questionnaire

These questions will help you develop your own questionnaire for your relatives or family friends. While some may not be applicable to all relatives or all families, we hope they will spark memories that help you on your journey of discovery. Type, or write these questions—and more of your own as they occur—on acid-free, lignin-free paper. Ask your relatives or family friends to fill it out. Be sure to provide enough space for answers. Send along an acid-free pen so that you can include the questionnaire in your album.

What is your full name? _____

Is there anything special or unusual about your name?_____

When and where were you born?_____

Do you have brothers and sisters? _____

What are their names and ages? _____

What are your parents' names? _____
_____

If they are not still living, when did they pass away?_____

Do you have more information about your family further back than your parents? _____
_____

What is your ethnic background? _____

Has it played an important role in your life?_____

Where did you live as a young child? _____

Where did you attend elementary school? _____

What year did you begin school? _____

Do you have any special memories from your elementary school days?_____

Where did you attend high school?_____

What year did you graduate?_____

Who were your best friends during high school? _____
_____
_____

Are you still in contact with them? _____
_____

What high school memories stand out in your mind? _____
_____
_____

What historical events took place during your school years? _____
_____
_____

How did they affect your family? _____
_____

After high school, did you attend college or vocational school? _____

What school did you attend, and what did you study? _____
_____

Did you serve in the Armed Forces? _____

If so, which branch of the service and what years? _____

What are your memories of your time in the service? _____

What was your first job?_____

What did you choose as your career?_____

Would you have changed anything regarding your career? _____

What is your spouse's name? _____

When and where did you meet? _____
_____
_____

Describe your courtship._____
_____
_____

When did you marry?_____

When was your first child born? _____
_____

How many children do you have? _____

What are their names? Ages? Where do they live? _____
_____
_____
_____
_____

What special memories of raising children would you like to share? _____
_____
_____

Do you enjoy traveling? _____

What has been your greatest travel adventure? _____
_____
_____
_____

Do you have hobbies? What are they?_____
_____

Do you belong to any organizations? Which ones? _____
_____
_____

Are you a grandparent? What is the best thing about being a grandparent? _____
_____
_____

If, knowing what you do now, you could change anything in your life, what would you change?
_____
_____

If you could do anything you wanted to right now, what would that be?_____
_____
_____

What do you feel is your greatest accomplishment?_____
_____
_____
_____

47

Glossary

Acid-free
Acid is used in paper manufacturing to break apart the wood fibers and the lignin which holds them together. If acid remains in the materials used for photo albums, the acid can react chemically with photographs and accelerate their deterioration. Acid-free products have a pH factor of 7.0 or above. It's imperative that all materials (glue, pens, paper, etc.) used in memory albums or scrapbooks be acid-free.

Acid migration
is the transfer of acidity from one item to another through physical contact or acidic vapors. If a newspaper clipping were put into an album, the area it touched would turn yellow or brown. A de-acidification spray can be used on acidic papers, or they can be color photocopied onto acid-free papers.

Archival quality
is a term used to indicate materials which have undergone laboratory analysis to determine that their acidic and buffered content is within safe levels.

Buffered Paper
During manufacture a buffering agent such as calcium carbonate or magnesium bicarbonate can be added to paper to neutralize acid contaminants. Such papers have a pH of 8.5.

Cropping
Cutting or trimming a photo to keep only the most important parts. See page 24 for cropping ideas and information about cropping Polaroid photos.

Journaling
refers to the text on a scrapbook page giving details about the photographs. Journaling can be done in your own handwriting or with adhesive letters, rub-ons, etc. It is probably the most important part of memory albums.

Lignin
is the bonding material which holds wood fibers together as a tree grows. If lignin remains in the final paper product (as with newsprint) it will become yellow and brittle over time. Most paper other than newsprint is lignin-free.

pH factor
refers to the acidity of a paper. The pH scale is the standard for measurement of acidity and alkalinity. It runs from 0 to 14 with each number representing a ten-fold increase; pH neutral is 7. Acid-free products have a pH factor from 7 or above. Special pH tester pens are available to help you determine the acidity or alkalinity of products.

Photo-safe
is a term similar to archival quality but more specific to materials used with photographs. Acid-free is the determining factor for a product to be labeled photo-safe.

Sheet protectors
These are made of plastic to slip over a finished album page. They can be side-loading or top-loading and fit 8½"x11" or 12"x12" pages. It is important that they be acid-free. Polypropylene (vinyl) is commonly used—never use these in your photo albums; they're not of archival quality.

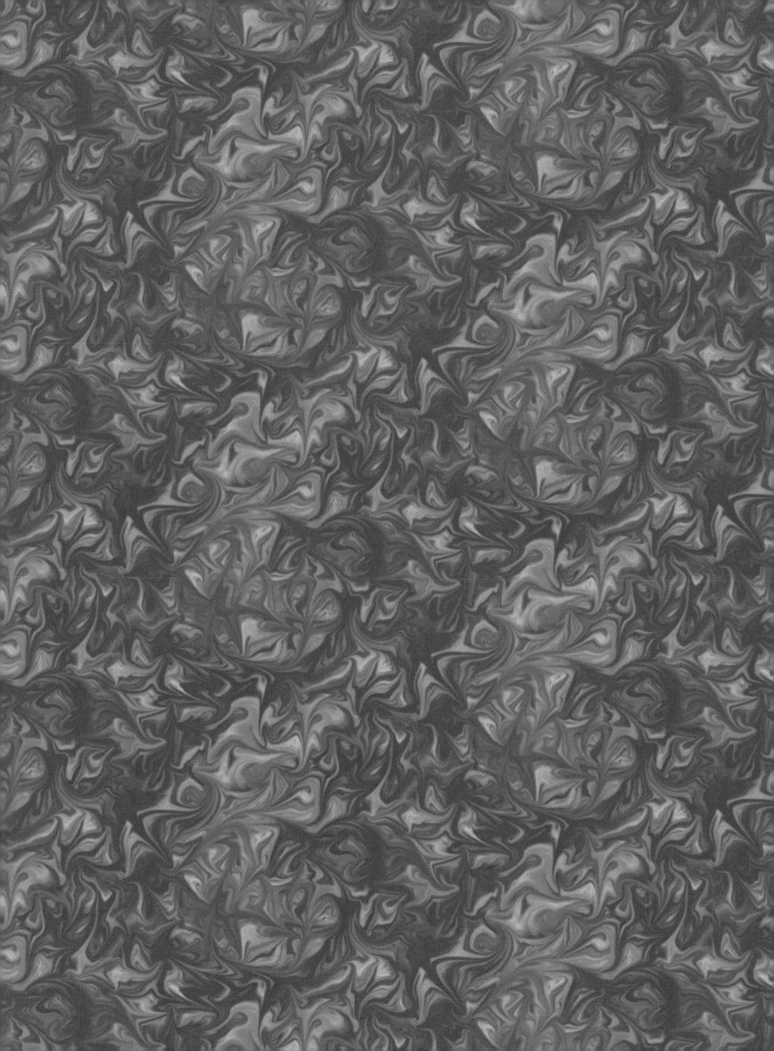

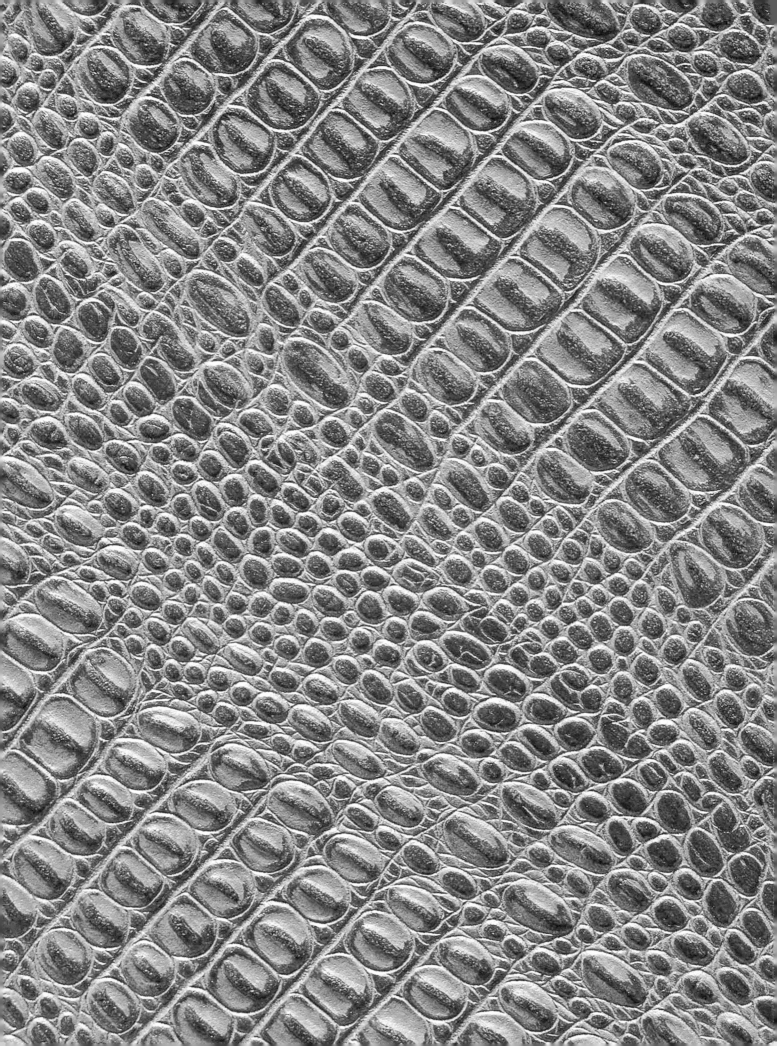